Jawaher Almulla was never one to talk much let alone talk about herself. She is simply a person that has gone through things that made her write her feelings down, transport all these emotions to paper and share them with people who will relate to them.

Writing was always an escape to her; never a necessity or a hobby. Just like travel is an escape to her where she takes herself out of whatever reality she's in and goes to that dreamlike state of high adrenalin and increased serotonin. She has travelled to over 30 countries and hopes that she can continue to discover new cultures and experience more adventures.

Jawaher has a very keen mind to learn and discover future innovations and to keep growing in her career. The same applies to her personal life; she likes to keep herself busy and active, juggling between kids, career, and personal predicaments.

To the person who loved from within, gave their heart away only to be returned shattered, left alone to pick up the pieces, the tiny shreds and the missing puzzles. It would take you a while but you will get there, keep looking and you will find new pieces along the way that will fit in that big heart of yours, just perfectly.

Jawaher Almulla

I Should Write This Down

Illustrated by Rashid Almulla

AUSTIN MACAULEY PUBLISHERS™
LONDON • CAMBRIDGE • NEW YORK • SHARJAH

ISBN – 9789948778165 – (Paperback)
ISBN – 9789948778172 – (E-Book)

Application Number: MC-10-01-6186807
Age Classification: E

Printer Name: iPrint Global Ltd
Printer Address: Witchford, England

First Published 2023
AUSTIN MACAULEY PUBLISHERS FZE
Sharjah Publishing City
P.O Box [519201]
Sharjah, UAE
Www.austinmacauley.ae
+971 655 95 202

On January 01, 2019 at 12:30 am, I wrote my first poem. Poems kept pouring through my heart, writing from a part of me that I never realized wanted to be heard. I knew then I should have written this down a long time ago.

Where It All Started

Sweet swift love,
Beating in the night
Gently caress the shores
Barely graze the soil

The worst kind of fantasy
The one you don't expect
The one that shrugs you hard
To pull you out of your head
And transport you down
From the galaxy far away, you were in
Eight years ago, it all started
Look how far away it soared
Oh, how far away it falls
Just let go
Don't bend for it any further
It ought to break your bones

Something was lost
Along the way
Over the horizons
Never returning
Possibly maybe
For eternity

I would like
More than anything in this world
To forget
To pretend
Like your words
Never cut through my heart
My wounds are too deep
That it is impossible
To forget

How am I supposed to go
Running after you
When you are standing behind
This raging fire
Let go of the notion
That I won't exist
If I don't sacrifice
Everything
To be with you

I'm starting over
Resetting the password
Flipping the page
Turning a new leaf
Out with the old
In with the new
Singing happy birthday
Blowing the candle
Wishing for a happier me

Here
Come again
Breath in this air
Bottle it up
Breath it again
Keep it in your lungs
For when you are wanderlust
It will remind you
Of the November autumn
That cool soft air

Deep down
She knew
It all unfolded the way
It was intended to be
Grievous
And sudden

I waited on the sidelines, a long cold night
Reminding myself, you will arrive
Five minutes, turned into thirty minutes,
Turned into one hour
Here you come and here I leave you
Cause I'm done waiting
For a shadow of a friend

It's the feeling of in-between
The feeling of hollow gaps
That extends its arms
And swallow you whole…
Listen
Try to live in that fog
It might spit you out
It might

Somehow in someway
I drifted too far
To realize the depth
In which I was falling
Somehow in someway
I lost my way to you
And I lost the map
That leads me back to you

Let the sunshine in
Invite the warmth
Let it seep into
Your skin
Rays engulfing your soul
Making you feel whole

The curse of hopeful minds
Is when you try to escape
To remember reality
It whispers in your ears
Everything will be okay

Through all these clouds
Shined one ray
Casting its light
On her bright eyes
With many dreams
Glistening inside.

I lay here wondering
Will I bear witness
To the unraveling world of mourning
Will I be tested
Given only to be taken
You
With your soft sweet words
Will I ever
Mourn over you

Soft calmness
Happy thoughts
The weight on my shoulder
Easing off with every stroke
Let me drift and lose all senses
This is my happy place

Brownie points
For every time I endure more
Your imagination
Is bigger than I could hold
So you keep slapping me with it
Asking me to stand still
Not move
So…
I do not move

Your mind
Is your greatest enemy
A lifelong battle that will
Alter the course of your world
Win it because you deserve it

Some words
Are like a knife
Into your flush
They will sting
They will leave a mark
They will have you
Eternally wounded

My fault
I did not recognize
The depth of your despair
The sickness of your mind
The twisted sides that you hide
So well,
I almost did not recognize

Palm trees
Low breeze
We ought to be free
Run wildly under the lights
Hear the squawks
Invite them in
Fear it not
I will be here
Caught in the dark

Alterations made
Stitches and seam
To fit a lifeless world
Which within we play
Tear those parts
Re stitch and relive
Design a fit perfect world
Which within you live

Wild life
Peace and quiet
She longs for it
To take care of herself
To feel the beauty of the world
To smell the trees and the ocean
To touch the sand
To free her mind
Of all burdens and attachments
She yearns for freedom

She said I found prince charming
She said I found the one
She said I think I will marry him
Maybe have his children
She said something is changing
Something is shifting
She said how come something so beautiful
Turn into what it is
She said little did I know
I'm already moving on

You reach your hands over
Caress the surface
Careful not to burst it
You tell yourself
This is what it means
To be high on life
Oh, how wondrous
Yet so skin-deep
My pleasure to acquaint with you Mr.
I'm afraid I did not like what I saw
So let me go ahead and burst that bubble
I prefer to live in the realm of sensibility

She keeps wandering
Back to that time
When everything was certain
And nothing was hopeless
Ran through the wild
Never looking back
Now she can't help
But stumble every mile

There is an emptiness
In this heart
That is about to explode
Turning its soul
Into fog and dust
Burning its ashes
To a pile of filth

Loneliness was on the verge
And desperation haunted me
Its grip woke me up
And put me back to sleep
It demanded that I move on
What left will never be the same
Desperation haunted me.
I answered to please let me be.

Sip the warmness
Let it seep through your veins
But be warned
It will make you forget
How you felt when he held your hands for the first time.
How your heartbeat thundered at the mention of his name.
How for a brief while it was all swans and doves.
Be warned.
Your veins will be empty again.

Calm thoughts
Sincere smile
Whatever I have known
Disappears with you
As though
I never lived before you
Never knew heartbreak
A newly born soul

Don't go far into the woods
Don't go deep into the murk
Take this rope and pull on now
Rise up, rise up, rise up
Open this cave and breath.
Just breath

It wasn't that long ago
That you believed in him
Saw the best
And it made you smile
Why though
It feels like a distant memory

You learn the hard way
The way life schemes
Tearful one second
And cheerful the next
Lessons learnt
Revise them well

Here I am
With a heavy heart
Declaring
That I no longer
Pledge my heart
To chasing shadows
To hopeless cases
To collecting
Scattered pieces
My life is mine
And only mine

Her soul won't fit everywhere
But where it fits
She will flourish

Something was said
Could not be unspoken
Harsh and cold
Numbed the feelings
Paralyzed
The air
They are breathing

Oh, how she fell from grace
She was high up there
Singing hallelujah
Dreaming of tomorrow
Tumble
Tumble
Tumble
Now burning in the sand

She lost her way
That year
When everything altered
New starts
Maybe sometimes are bad starts
To something you so long longed for
Unbeknownst to you
The results will carry the good
That you will live up
And will carry the bad
That will crush you down
Hopeful as ever
Wishful
Carry on

She hears a humming
And her head is swaying
Light as a feather
Lost in the melody
It's the sound of life
Music to her ears
Of everything around her
Alive and well

She felt the rain on her cheeks
Drowning beneath her skin
She knew that those sky tears
Will feed her joyful soul
So every time the sky cries
She dances to its tune.

How It All Ends

This is the life
We expected
We lived
We survived
Tears shed
And hearts broken
Twisted worlds
Collided
And we are free
At last

Sore eyes
And heavy hearts
Anxious feelings
And distant voices
Breaking her slowly
Word by word
Telling her to regret
All the choices she has made
No options were spared
Only blame and guilt remain

Envy hearts
Stealing our life
Making us blind
To what we have
Carries a weight
Heavier than bricks

Happiness is long gone
Behind words
Not spoken
Behind tears
Wiped out on our pillow
Wearing us down
Leaving us crippled
Happiness is no longer
In sight

Blue and white skies
Green and pink gardens
Brown and blue beaches
White and black mountains
Imagine it all in my head
Paint it all in my canvas
Transport it down in my world
Here in my old couch

What it feels to have memories?
Like this cavity that you can't get rid of
Like this stain on your rug that won't wash off
Like this white hair that will keep reappearing
When the dye is off
Memories always there
Hard to scrub off

It is your undoing
Undoing the love
Digging up the dirt's
Removing the roots
Trashing what's left
Of this dying plumeria
Planting new seeds
Of purple heart

Memories flooded my brain
Heart grew heavier
Tears fell down
And if tears
Could bring back
All the memories
Who would we be now?

Temporary love
And temporary pain
Move the feelings away
Silence the horror inside
It all shall end anyway
Temporary things
And temporary life

Begging
The selfish heart
To take my hand
Take me whole
But don't stand like stone
Cold hearted.
Realizing
I'm begging
A wall

Selfishness
What led you here
Tearing those hearts apart
Thinking they are fine
Cause selfishness
Festered into your brain
Laid eggs and took residence
Into what once was peace

Endless possibilities
For hope and glory
To raise a new roof
And bring up
Generation of rays
Into the atmosphere
Carrying smiles and strength

This silence is demeaning
Taking a horrible feeling
Twisting and churning it
Leaving this soul empty
No resolution
Or meaning
Just a lonely place
Where the silence is beaming

Suppose we never met
On that fateful day
When you eyed me from across the room
Remembered my name and my seat
Fate worked in a mysterious way
So, you pretended to forget my name
Just to get the pace going
Suppose I didn't fall for all of that
Suppose we left the grounds
Like the strangers we came
Our worlds upside down
Yours is up
Mine is down
Walking in parallel
Never in the same verse
But I suppose fate wanted a heartbreak.

Dear Saint Helena[1],
Kindly deliver this message,
To the person who has been
Harboring this heart
For too long.
Let them know
A new ship will sail soon,
The kind of ship
That will bring joy
To this island.
They ought to know,
This heart suffered enough
But it is beating again.
My best Regards,

---

[1] The Saint Helena hoopoe, also known as the Saint Helena giant hoopoe or giant hoopoe, is an extinct species of the hoopoe, known exclusively from an incomplete subfossil skeleton. It was last seen around 1550.

It is a simple life
Simply twisted
Into simple knots
With simple loops and
Simple bends
It is a simple life
That's hard to navigate

Uncertainty is
A dark fog
Burning your flush
In contact
Step into the uncertain future
And there is no way back
Take small steps
Scabs will form
Time will heal
With no fast forward
But until then
Navigate through the dark fog

It's one of those days
Weighted down by the memory
Of the old house
Bustling inside
The big windows
Overlooking the ocean
The small town
Where I left a piece
Of my heart
Thought I will come back
To pick it up
Now I'm here
The piece is there
The distance is vast
And the memories are heavy

Would you believe me if I said?
It's in all in your head
The made-up fictions
And the horrible fabrications
Would you believe me if I begged you?
To hear the truth in my voice
Ditch the fictions
And listen to my words
Nowhere near reality
Is the image you paint
Of me and my world

She Wandered around
Through the valleys and back
Leaving a piece of trail
For the time she will come back
Sooner than ever
She will be back

Take me whole
Don't leave me skin and bone
The mess I have endured
From all the back and forth
Left me in the drought
So much pain to go through
You didn't care
The skin is not yours
And the bones aren't strong

How delusional
Believing in this mirage
From a distance
All the optical
Too good to be true
Was I fool
Believing in all that shiny gold
Or was I a hopeless dreamer

The path to new horizons
Start with this step
Set your heart free
And your mind will follow
Make new promises
Your old self could not keep
Something good
And something magical
Will flow along the path

Changes have flown over my head
Unnoticeable to my lonely eyes
Creeped up, up my spine
Trickled into my brain
Too late to medicate
No way to sedate

As I depart
From this flight
I realize
The great divine
Of those
Who departed before us
And those who
Never arrived
Their footprints
Left in the hallways
And their voices
Echoes in the lounges

Cause we be going
Through minutes and hours
Concealing
What we think
We do not feel
Until we hear
That song
That sends the tears
Drifting down
Like rain
Then we realize
We do not feel
What we think
We feel

This place is not mine
Without you in it
Every corner is casting
Your shadow
Reminding me of us
Can't escape this feeling
Take your shadow with you
And leave
It is haunting me
Night and day

Regret is what brought me
Back here to your door
Forgiven and forgotten
Wish I heard those words
Embraced in the warmth of love
Given what was lacking
Reality was never my friend
The door remained closed

I'm laying here
Counting the stars
You are sleeping
Living the good life
Differences
Grew us apart
It's been like that
For a while
So, tell me how to find
The thread
That connects us
Cause promises were made
To never turn your back
But here we are
Back-to-back
Me counting the stars
You sound a sleep

How long will I miss you?
Somewhere in between tomorrow and forever
Possibly when the heart stop
Slowly leaving this soul
And the eyes dry out
While the veins get clogged
From the pressure of the force
Of the feeling of longing
And there is no tomorrow
And no hope of forever

So, you say you want to talk
About the things you never could
All of this burden inside
Too heavy to keep locked
You want it to be known
That your heart is full
Of heartaches and disappointments
Caused by your fragile feelings
You want to vent and mend
Therapy to your soul
So, say what you want to say
If it will fix your broken heart

How did you come here?
Which door led you to this gate
Kept it close for too long
No soul knocked on it before
Came out of nowhere
Hopeless and bored
Save me from this misery
Echoed across the halls
Love me like never before
Come to my dark passages
And light them with your glimmer

Ending a dead-end
Before hitting that spot
Cause you know it is not,
And it won't be.
Hard as it may seem, the wisest choice.

One day it will happen
You even know it
This heart of yours
Will grow and become full
Seemingly bursting
With fireworks
And butterflies
So happy and giddy
With the mention
Of a name

Some type of void
Is filled with your love
Warm and fuzzy
Blanket to my heart
Past heartbreaks
Mended and forgotten
Like they never
Resided in the same void

Misunderstood
Faking things to get ahead
Pretending to be
What appears to be
Strong and confident
That is just a façade
That I laid ahead of me
Never my intention
To hurt a fragile soul
Deep regrets
Are set in my heart
Sorry seems to be
The only word

I was your beam
Supporting your wall
Carrying the heavy weight
Unburdened by it all
Until it came down
Crashing on my heart
Breaking every piece of me
Realizing too late
That the burden was there
All along
Just suppressed
By my love

This pit in my stomach
I placed it in there
Stupid decisions
And lonely feelings
Will regret them
And will change
But this pit
Won't go away

They say
Blink and it is gone
But I have blinked
A thousand time
To see the world disappear
Vanish before my eyes
Reality remained
And eventually
My eyes
Stopped.

This dream of mine
To have you all my life
Impossible to attain
So fast to vanish
Like a gust of wind
That came to relieve me
From the scorching sun
But the wind blew fast
And blew all the dreams with it.